THE ROOM
WHERE IT
HPPENS

T0206716

THE ROOM WHERE IT H★PPENS

A Lent course for groups or individuals based on the musical
HAMILTON

BISHOP ROSE HUDSON-WILKIN

DARTON · LONGMAN + TODD

First published in 2021 by
Darton, Longman and Todd Ltd
1 Spencer Court
140 – 142 Wandsworth High Street
London SW18 4JJ

ISBN: 978-1-913657-78-9

A catalogue record for this book is available from the
British Library.

Printed and bound in Great Britain by Bell & Bain, Glasgow

PUBLISHER'S NOTE

The Room Where it Happens is a course intended for Lenten study over five weeks, ideally for use in small groups although it can be adapted for personal use by an individual reader. The course is based on themes derived from the stage musical *Hamilton*. When this book was commissioned, it was expected that a DVD of the filmed presentation of the musical would be commercially available by the time it was published. However, the release of this DVD has been delayed and, at the time of going to press, there has been no indication that it is likely to be available before the start of the season of Lent in 2022. Until it becomes available, a little bit of creative resourcefulness will be necessary!

For example, the film is available to watch through the Disney+ subscription service (for which the price of a one- or two-month subscription is likely to be less than the cost of a DVD). Each of the clips from *Hamilton* that Bishop Rose suggests you watch is one of the songs from the musical and can be found on the album of the original Broadway cast recording. Many other resources can be found online.

I am sincerely grateful to David Moloney for believing that I could do this, and to Kenneth my husband and Sandye my Spiritual Director for their constant encouragement.

CONTENTS

INTRODUCTION

The popularity of the musical *Hamilton* took the world of theatre-goers by storm and made a big impact. Our interest in the historical figure of Alexander Hamilton has been stirred up in a new and fresh way. Who was this man? Why were people willing to queue up around the block to see this production? Why were the cast of the show invited by US President Barack and First Lady Mrs Michelle Obama to put on an exclusive performance at the White House? You can imagine the joy I felt when my daughter called to say that she was able to get me tickets for *Hamilton* and I was therefore able to see it, to experience this phenomenon for myself. I found it refreshing to be sitting in a packed, mainstream theatre in London's West End, watching a story unfold in high-energy, hip-hop music and with such a diverse set of performers as well as a diverse audience. It was evident that this genre of music attracted a new and much younger audience than most traditional musicals. I am personally excited at the possibility of exploring some of the themes drawn from *Hamilton* as we begin our Lenten journey together.

Hamilton is a musical that tells the story of a young immigrant who migrated to the United States of America, overcoming his tragic beginnings and becoming engaged in the political life of his new country. A large part of Alexander Hamilton's education came from the 'school of life'. He knew what he believed in, and this became the foundation of his ambition: to achieve more and to be the best that he could be. As a child he saw people of African origin being enslaved and, in his heart, he believed that to be wrong but was hardly in a position to change the injustices that he witnessed. When he was no longer just an orphan child, he recognised that he *could* make a difference. He knew that staying silent was not an option. In an early exchange with his new-found, friend, Aaron Burr, shortly after arriving in the United States, Hamilton is recorded as saying, 'If you stand for nothing, what will you fall for?'

This musical is set within the hip-hop tradition, which naturally attracts a younger audience and therefore provides a 'homely' context in which we can engage and learn as a community – such as a family group, a church home group, or a church youth group – on a weekly basis during Lent. During the five weeks of the Lenten season, this course will draw on a number of *Hamilton's* most pertinent themes, namely: *Identity and Belonging, Ambition and Temptation, Forgiveness and Redemption, Love and Sacrifice* and *Hope and Courage through Adversity*. The title of this book, *The Room Where it Happens*, is an invitation to all of us to be present and engaged – whether in a front room, a church, or a village hall – as we discuss these life-giving themes. Let us be in the room where it is happening.

I am reminded that many years ago, when I worked as an associate priest at the Church of the Good Shepherd in West Bromwich, in the West Midlands, my work took me into local schools. I recall one of those schools having a Sikh headmaster. They had a school population of approximately 85 per cent Muslim and Sikh, and 15 per cent Afro-Caribbean and white working-class background. While conducting assembly in that school during the Lenten season, I noticed that the Muslim children were the most animated as they responded to questions about the meaning and practice of Lent. As a Christian priest, I found the religious literacy and fluency amongst those Muslim primary age-group children very interesting. I watched and listened as they comfortably linked the Lenten season to their own observance of Ramadan and their practice of fasting.

In my conversations with the children, I recognised that their knowledge and religious practice around Ramadan (and hence their interpretation of Lent) was not only learnt from a taught environment (such as school and mosque), but that the home played an equally important role. Faith was being practised within the home, in community, as well. Similarly, this Lent course seeks to encourage faith learning from within the multiple communities to which we belong: our home, our schools and our friendship circles. It invites family and friends to share freely around some of the strong themes that matter in our lives; themes to do with the messages that come from within and around us about our identity, who we think we are, and the way we are treated by others that challenge the very nature of our being and our sense of belonging. *The Room Where it Happens* invites us to make connections between some of the great theological themes, such as temptation, forgiveness, love, sacrifice and hope, and our everyday lives. It is my hope that, like the young Muslim children in the primary school from my parish back in the West Midlands, we will find ourselves at the end of the course more literate and fluent when it comes to expressing our faith, and comfortable and willing, not only to recognise, but to speak about the difference faith is making in our daily living.

Further, it is my hope that those engaging with this Lenten study will not only include children and young people in the group but will be able to draw on the contributions that they bring to the table. This will mean intentionally including those of a younger age group and enabling the kind of mutual learning where the contribution of all is valued, leading to a growth in confidence and a further growth in our faith literacy and fluency – the kind of growth that will see us relaxed and at ease as we navigate living out our faith in our homes, the places where we work or play, and beyond the walls of our church buildings.

HOW TO USE THIS BOOK

You have chosen this book based on the movie of the stage production of *Hamilton* for your Lenten pilgrimage, so let's RISE UP and get started! To get the best from this Lenten journey, I would encourage you to have a pre-session gathering before Week One begins so that everyone has the chance to view the movie in its entirety (it is approximately two and a half hours long). For that viewing, be ready with your Lent book, a notepad and pen. Some people may want to watch it twice (either before or after the group viewing) and if that is possible, I would encourage that. The musical setting of the production is hip-hop – a genre of music that most of our young people will be very much at home with. If any member of the group finds this musical style outside of their comfort zone, they may appreciate the second viewing. It will mean that by the time you get around to watching the suggested clips together as a group each week, everyone should be well tuned in to hearing the words being sung, connecting with the many different characters and their individual stories, and the film's message, tapping their feet and singing along.

The Room Where it Happens is a course divided into five sessions with the intention for it to be used weekly in preparation for Holy Week and Easter. Realistically, allocating two hours every week should allow for each session to be unhurried. It is especially important for the group leader to familiarise themselves with the material and to decide, knowing their group, how best to frame the suggested questions, including knowing which of the questions would be the best prompter to engage the group in conversation. It may become apparent that as a group you have other questions that you wish to grapple with and, if this is so, I would encourage you not to be afraid to give priority to those questions, setting aside the suggested ones. It would be of equal value if every individual taking part were to read the material weekly in advance of each session. As the group leader may not get to cover everything in the session due to time constraints, members of the group may want to go over the reading material for themselves and feel how it sits with them.

Although this musical is energetic and gets us moving our feet and bodies to the rhythm of the beat, we must not forget that we are being guided through Lent. It is important to note that we are not being called to be in a place of darkness during the season. Instead, we are being called each week to take our turn to walk towards the light; to investigate the mirror – it's a Jesus mirror. In looking at the mirror we get to see the light – to see Jesus. We get to see and name who we are. We get to see the things around us that we have allowed to shape us. In looking into this mirror, we get to see something of the light of Christ that we are all being called to and drawn by, and we get to acknowledge all that we can be in Christ.

Each week the sessions will begin and end with prayer. Let's use these moments to gird ourselves and each other as we prepare to speak the truth to one another about the journey we are on and the challenges along the way. We gird ourselves as we remember when we have allowed the things that others say about us to take centre stage, pushing Christ to the fringes, and we gird ourselves as, in the strength of Christ, we stand (rise up), ready to walk in the light and strength of God.

WEEK ONE

'My name is':
Identity and Belonging

GENESIS 1:26A, 27, 31A

Then God said, 'Let us make humankind in our image, according to our likeness; …' So God created humankind in his image, in the image of God he created them; male and female he created them. … God saw everything that he had made, and indeed, it was very good.

PRAYER

Creator God, we thank you that you have made us in your own image. When life experiences leave us feeling less than a valued part of your creation, help us to remember that you were pleased with your handiwork. May we also be reminded that you were despised and rejected. You experienced sorrow and grief, so you can understand when we feel rejected; you can feel our sorrow and our sadness. We thank you for your presence with us in our valleys of darkness. Help us to keep our eyes on you and your everlasting goodness. AMEN.

INTRODUCTION

With the explosion of social media, it has become somewhat a part of our reality that many of our identities are forged or broken in the digital world. I am sure we have heard stories, and not just from young people, of those whose identity has become tied up in the numbers of followers they have or with the messages that come into their homes through the medium of social media. We have learnt of stories of self-harm resulting from individuals being trolled, or of people being tricked as others have pretended to be what or who they are not, resulting in damaging consequences. I have heard people recount how ashamed they were to let people know that they had allowed themselves to be conned, afraid that they would look even more foolish. We find ourselves harbouring and sometimes expressing fear about what 'other people', who we may not even have met, think of us.

SHARE AND DISCUSS

Choose two or three people within the group to share briefly a story they have been aware of about the negative impact of social media. This might be something about which they have personal knowledge – to do with a family member, a friend, or even a story relating to themselves. For example, like me, some of you may have heard accounts of very young children feeling coerced into sending images of themselves over the internet.

Discuss briefly what we are hearing and what we make of these stories.

At the very start of *Hamilton* the musical, we get our first introduction to Hamilton the person. We may already be quite intrigued by this historical figure or have conjured up a variety of thoughts about him based on certain assumptions and expectations of what we have heard others say. Like all historical figures, we can only actually meet him through other people's eyes. On this occasion we are meeting Alexander Hamilton through the eyes of Lin-Manuel Miranda. Whoever the eyes belong to, and whatever the lens, we will all need to draw on our imaginations and transport ourselves to the Caribbean island of Nevis in the mid- to late-eighteenth century; to be outraged by the behaviour and attitudes of some while being bemused by others and, all the time, to conjure up our own thoughts about this character and his amazing accomplishments. His name is Alexander Hamilton!

As this is our first week in Lent, I would like to enter Hamilton's story by looking at the central character in the Lenten story – Jesus. I cannot help but wonder what Jesus must have been feeling and thinking about some of the rumours and half-truths that were being spread about him. Did he feel a sense of despair that the people (and sometimes even the disciples) just didn't get it? Was he tired of having to set the record straight time and time again? It can get wearisome constantly having to put across who you are and why you are doing what you are doing. An additional difficulty for Jesus was that in his time there were no PR companies or communications departments to speak on his behalf. The disciples may have been his friends, but he was always having to explain things to them. An example of this is seen in the story of the Sower and the Seeds (Matt. 13).

BIBLE

Let us now read from Matthew's gospel about a conversation that Jesus had with his disciples as he wrestled with what people may or may not have been saying about who he was and how he was being represented.

Choose two different people to read this passage, with a short pause between the two readings.

MATTHEW 16:13–17

Now when Jesus came into the district of Caesarea Philippi, he asked his disciples, 'Who do people say that the Son of Man is?' And they said, 'Some say John the Baptist, but others Elijah, and still others Jeremiah or one of the prophets.' He said to them, 'But who do you say that I am?' Simon Peter answered, 'You are the Messiah, the Son of the living God.' And Jesus answered him, 'Blessed are you, Simon son of Jonah! For flesh and blood has not revealed this to you, but my Father in heaven.'

Now that you have heard the passage twice, consider what words and phrases stood out for you and why.

THINK AND DISCUSS

Take around 15 minutes to discuss the following questions. If you are in a large group, it might be better to split into pairs or groups of three.

Have you ever heard yourself ask one of the following questions?

1. **Who do you think I am?**
2. **Why do I feel like I do not belong in this place?**
3. **Why do I not feel like I am a part of this group?**
4. **Why do I not feel like I am not accepted in this family?**

Spend a moment thinking about experiences you have been through which left you with that sense of being uncertain, or feeling that you were not accepted or that you did not belong. Have you ever walked into a room and, because of the reactions of those in the room, wondered what people were saying about you? Perhaps they were not even looking in your direction but something inside your very being told you they were talking about you. How were you left feeling? And how could you comfortably re-engage within that setting?

It may be of some assurance that Jesus (the human person) was beginning to wonder what people may be saying about him at this point in his life. Were they thinking of him as an 'upstart rabble rouser'? Was he just thought of as the carpenter's son and therefore, 'What could he possibly have to say that would be of more importance than the upstanding and well-known Scribes and Pharisees?' Jesus is perhaps wrestling with his own thoughts on the matter before deciding to test out on his friends the question, 'Who do people say that I am?' How we see Jesus, who we deem him to be, will make the difference in how we respond to Jesus or even relate to him. The disciples responded to Jesus by telling him what they heard other people saying. 'Some say you are John the Baptist, but others say Elijah…' Then Jesus asked the critical question, 'What about you, who do you say that I am?' It is much easier for us to repeat the things we hear other people saying, and we often do so without any sense of responsibility regarding the message we're passing on – as if it has nothing to do with us. But now the ball is in our court, and we are called to give an account of our own views. Will we be as open and honest with what we have been thinking all along? Peter is quick off the mark, and he answers first: 'You are the Messiah, the Son of the living God.' This answer is a real game-changer. You see, we relate and respond to others depending on what we think about them and who we think they are.

WATCH

Let's now look at our first video clip from the musical. In this clip, Alexander Hamilton wants everyone to know who he is right from the start. Perhaps he wants them to know that whatever they may have heard, they should judge him not by that but by their direct dealings with him. They may have heard about his past, where he came from. He now wants them to know who he is presently more than how his life may have begun.

Show video clip of the song 'Alexander Hamilton'.

The story of Alexander Hamilton, described in this musical production, begins with an unflattering description of his start in life: 'a bastard, orphan, son of a whore…, in effect, a nobody and not just any nobody – to top it off, he is an immigrant.' That Hamilton was repeatedly taunted with this from childhood would have no doubt left him feeling a sense of insecurity; this insecurity was apparent throughout the rest of his comparatively short life. His childhood in the Caribbean was marred by poverty and broken family relationships. He was brought up by his mother and, when she died, life as an orphan left him unprotected and therefore even more vulnerable. Stories of his childhood give us a picture of a mother who had tried to protect both him and his siblings, and a resilient young man, intelligent, keen to learn and well-read.

After a hurricane in Nevis, he was assisted to migrate to the USA and although he quickly made friends there, one gets a sense that he was held at arm's length. He was viewed as 'not one of us'; he was, after all, 'an immigrant', and what would he know or have to offer of any real significance?

There is much in Hamilton's story that resonates with me. My older sister and I were born out of wedlock and, when I was approximately two years old, my mother left us behind in Jamaica and travelled to England. There was nothing unusual about this, as thousands of other families also made similar journeys. I suspect that when my parents parted, there may have been plans for my father to join her and then for us to follow later. After all, this was the well-worn path that many followed from the Caribbean: one parent going first, followed by another and then the children. My father, however, showed no interest in 'making an honest woman' of my mother (marrying her). It meant that she took matters into her own hands. Not long after she arrived in England, she met and married a tall, dashing, athletically built young man and they soon started a new family. Back in Jamaica where my sister and I were growing up, although we were cared for by my aunt, my father's sister, there were numerous times that I can remember feeling like I did not belong, times when I did feel forgotten. I can still vividly remember how this felt. Perhaps it was in some of the tasks that my sister and I were given to do that I noticed others within the family belonged more than we did. Looking back now, it could simply have been that being the youngest in the family we drew the short straw for all the unpalatable jobs around the house. Or perhaps it was the constant reminder that my aunt had the added responsibility of taking care of us that jarred me even at so young an age.

I learnt years later that my grandmother, my father's mother, had left Cuba during the height of the unrest under Fidel Castro's presidency with her five children (three daughters and two sons). The hardship had taken its toll on her, and she became mentally unwell and could no longer care for them. In effect, my father and his siblings grew themselves up! They were Spanish-speaking Cubans, now trying to assimilate as patois (broken dialect)-speaking Jamaicans. Who were they truly? Looking back, I can see the scars, and I note that the emotional and psychological scars were greater, because those scars were deeply embedded in the psyche of my father and his siblings, and we somehow found them still rearing their ugly heads from time to time, as if implanted in our DNA.

The new acquaintances of Alexander Hamilton in the USA were pondering: 'Who is this guy?' He was from an impoverished place, and had no father to endow him with wealth and guidance like his friends had. From all that they had heard of the Caribbean being 'a forgotten place', how did he make it to the place where he was now? Perhaps the answer lies in this very first song: he was exposed to things that no child should ever see ('*slaves being slaughtered and carted away*'); but ('*he struggled and kept his guard up, he was longing for something inside to be a part of*'). To come through all this, to know (according to the history books) that he was in effect being punished by not being accepted in mainstream school (run nevertheless by the Church) because his parents were unmarried, would have also given him another 'stripe' that could easily have pushed him over the edge. But instead, we see such resilience!

A hurricane of some magnitude struck and devastated the island. This could have been the last straw but he 'rises up'! He wrote a letter telling his story, many local people caught a glimpse of something special in this young boy, and money was collected to send him away so that his life was not further devastated by the after-effects of the hurricane. There was something almost prophetic about the actions of those who saved him captured in the words, '*Get your education, don't forget from whence you came, and the world is gonna know your name.*' Growing up in Jamaica, my semi-illiterate folks also used to say to us, 'Get yourself an education because when you have it, nobody can take it away from you.'

So how do we treat those who we deem not to have had a privileged upbringing? In Britain we have much to say about class – upper class, middle class and working class. And I guess we say 'working class' because it would not be politically correct to openly say 'lower class'. Coming from a place of real poverty in the Caribbean myself, I cannot help but think of the lives of the many 'Alexander Hamiltons' who have been swept away by various devastating experiences; the many 'Alexander Hamiltons' who have since made their way to the USA, Britain and Western Europe, who are not seen as individuals with something to offer to their new adopted country, but instead seen in a derogatory way, a drain on that society. Those people travel thousands of miles to make a better life, arriving with hopes and dreams waiting to be fulfilled. However, they are not welcomed; they are looked down on with suspicion, locked away in detention centres, and called unpleasant names – names which means 'you are of very little value', or 'you are not of much worth'.

BIBLE

Let's read another passage of Scripture, this time from the Old Testament. In this passage, like the Children of Israel, we are being reminded that we too have been a 'pilgrim people' (a 'wandering Aramean'). If we have not moved ourselves, then our forebears have moved. What was our experience of arriving in our new place? Who were the people that played a part in helping us to settle in, that helped to get the best from us? Think about what life would be like if we were called names and treated as outcasts. What would that do to our mental wellbeing?

Choose two different people to read this passage, with a short pause between the two readings.

DEUTERONOMY 26:1–11
When you have come into the land that the LORD your God is giving you as an inheritance to possess, and you possess it, and settle in it, you shall take some of the first of all the fruit of the ground, which you harvest from the land that the LORD your God is giving you, and you shall put it in a basket and go to the place that the LORD your God will choose as a dwelling for his name. You shall go to the priest

who is in office at that time, and say to him, 'Today I declare to the LORD your God that I have come into the land that the LORD swore to our ancestors to give us.' When the priest takes the basket from your hand and sets it down before the altar of the LORD your God, you shall make this response before the LORD your God: 'A wandering Aramean was my ancestor; he went down into Egypt and lived there as an alien, few in number, and there he became a great nation, mighty and populous. When the Egyptians treated us harshly and afflicted us, by imposing hard labour on us, we cried to the LORD, the God of our ancestors; the LORD heard our voice and saw our affliction, our toil, and our oppression. The LORD brought us out of Egypt with a mighty hand and an outstretched arm, with a terrifying display of power, and with signs and wonders; and he brought us into this place and gave us this land, a land flowing with milk and honey. So now I bring the first of the fruit of the ground that you, O LORD, have given me.' You shall set it down before the LORD your God and bow down before the LORD your God. Then you, together with the Levites and the aliens who reside among you, shall celebrate with all the bounty that the LORD your God has given to you and to your house.

Now that you have heard the passage twice, consider what words and phrases stood out for you and why.

Since time immemorial, people have moved from their country of origin due to acts of war, natural disasters, or simply to make a better life for themselves (for health reasons, or to improve the financial position for them and their family). The British were masterful in their colonisation project. They did not move because of war or natural disaster but they were in effect economic migrants, seeking to amass wealth. Churchill is alleged to have said that it was Britain's ownership of the Caribbean that gave them the resources needed for the war. It is fair to say too that Britain has welcomed, at different stages, waves of different immigrant communities: Jews fleeing the Holocaust post-war Caribbeans, Ugandan Asians, and more recently those fleeing the Chinese regime in Hong Kong.

THINK AND DISCUSS

Discuss the following questions as a group.

1. **How do we as a community enable newcomers (sometimes referred to as 'incomers') to feel a sense of belonging?**
2. **When we hear negative things being said about newcomers, do we silently collude, or do we intervene, saying what we believe to be right?**

The passage in Deuteronomy reminds us that fruits reaped are to be shared with all, including those deemed to be 'aliens'. Other passages in the Bible give similar encouragements to landowners; for example:

'When you reap the harvest of your land, you shall not reap to the very edges of your field, or gather the gleanings of your harvest; you shall leave them for the poor and for the alien' (Lev. 23:22). Many who migrate to new countries tell a different story to what we often hear from our tabloid press.

In verses 5 to 10 of Deuteronomy 26, we find what can be described as a sort of recitation reminding the Israelites of where they are coming from and what God had done for them. I wonder if we have a sense of what God has done for us, or a sense of where we are coming from, or even of the journey that we are on. As we travel in life, what do we recite? What are the things that we replay in our minds about the journey we have been on, where we are coming from, or even where we want to go? Could it be that, if we had had this inner practice of recitation, remembering our own journeys and that of our forebears, we might be more sympathetic to those we now refer to as refugees and immigrants who are seeking to come to our shores?

There is something both implicit and explicit about naming the issue of how we need to show care for those who are most vulnerable, those who comes to our countries and are not able initially to care for themselves. The name-calling that Alexander Hamilton experienced would have further damaged his sense of identity. This could possibly have fuelled his need to prove himself (to be like Aaron Burr). From his story in the first song, we can see that he wanted people to know who he was. And what is equally important is that he did not want to sit on the sidelines. He wanted actively to be at home in his new country and that would also mean being engaged with the topics of the day; for Hamilton, the main topics were the civil war and the enslavement of Africans. He knew that he was good with words, and he used this gift of words to encourage others to join the revolutionary movement; to make a difference and to be the change they wanted to see.

WATCH

Hamilton signposts from the beginning his great desire to improve himself. He gets it. He knows that his education will play a vital role in all of this. In this next video clip, we find him enquiring of Aaron Burr how he might be able to take an accelerated course to qualify earlier. 'I hear you did some accelerated learning. I want to go down that same route too.'

Show video clip of the song 'My Shot'.

Although he was being verbally abused, Hamilton was single-minded in his efforts to be accepted into the fold of this new country. The dreams and hopes of those who have made long journeys, seeking refuge from natural disasters or from wars, deserve to be given the space in which those people can find themselves, adapt to their new environment and begin to build a future. How, as a Christian community, might we be able to ensure that others not only feel welcome but are able to find work so that they can provide for themselves and their families? Helping them to regain their sense of dignity as human beings would be the best welcome that could be extended to those who come to us as refugees or seeking asylum.

A few years ago, I was invited to address American Service personnel based in England, at a Thanksgiving Service at one of our cathedrals. Someone from the base began by saying that when the British came to America, 'they were pilgrims and pioneers'. No reference to them being economic migrants, seeking to improve their financial wellbeing. I recall gulping at the thought that, today, many trying to reach those same shores are referred to in a less charitable way. As I write this Lent book, news has been broken that the Duke of Edinburgh has died. The airwaves are full of stories of his life, and it has caught my attention that at a very young age he too was in effect brought to this country in the capacity of someone needing refuge, while still a baby.

Nearly one hundred years later, the world is still grappling with large movements of people due to serious unrest caused by governments failing to respect the human rights of all its citizens. We desperately need to see a new kind of leadership in the United Nations, the G7 and the Commonwealth. The kind of leadership that will enable us to recognise the loss of the gifts that refugees could potentially bring to their adopted country, not to mention the loss to their own country of origin. We may also ponder the psychological trauma that seeps into the DNA of so many refugees, and that many struggle later in life with issues of identity and belonging. This kind of struggle impacts on the wider community. Both Alexander Hamilton and the Duke of Edinburgh were very gifted men who did not throw their hands up in despair at their challenging beginnings; neither 'threw away their shot'. They found a way to give back – to commit themselves to serving others; to find themselves; to belong.

REFLECTION

As this first session draws to a close, let's pause and call to mind who we are as children of the one heavenly Father. Let us reaffirm that our identity is interlocked with others; we do not stand alone. We think of the Zulu word, *Ubuntu* – 'I am because you are.' Let us recommit ourselves to positively enabling one another to feel a sense of belonging to each other and to the communities of which we are a part. Whatever our beginnings, let us remind ourselves and each other that we have the potential to become that which we aspire to be.

PRAYER

Dear Lord, I am only a spark; open my eyes that I may see the fire I can become, giving warmth to others. I am only a string; enable me to envision the instrument – (for example, the lyre) to which I belong and the accompanying strings which, together, make beautiful music. I am only a drop; make me connect with your life-giving fountain that satisfies all our thirst. I am only a feather; help me play my part and take flight on the wings of a dove to share your everlasting peace. May I always rest assured in the knowledge that along with all God's creation, I am beautifully and wonderfully made in your image. **Amen.**

Together, each in our own language, let us say the prayer Jesus taught us:

Our Father, who art in heaven, hallowed be thy name; thy kingdom come; thy will be done on earth as it is in heaven. Give us this day our daily bread; and forgive us our trespasses as we forgive those who trespass against us; and lead us not into temptation but deliver us from evil. For thine is the kingdom, the power, and the glory. For ever and ever. **Amen.**

ACTION

In the light of what you have learnt this week, what will you do differently, or take forward?

PRAYER

Lord, teach me to **strive to be in the room** where we recognise and affirm each other's sense of belonging and the gifts we all bring to the table.

WEEK TWO

'Rise Up':
Ambition and Temptation

PHILIPPIANS 3:13b–14

But one thing I do: forgetting what is behind and straining towards what is ahead, I press on towards the goal to win the prize for which God has called me heavenwards in Christ Jesus. (NIV)

PRAYER

Dear Lord, there is so much I want to do, to see, to achieve to become the best that I can be. Help me in this quest that my achievements will not be gained at another's expense. Grant me a spirit of generosity that I may not possess the gifts that you have given me but willingly use them for the benefit of the wider community. Remove from me the temptation of self-importance that leads me away from you, and give me the humility which allows me to admit my errors of judgement and to be always ready to be reconciled to you and others. **Amen**.

INTRODUCTION

As a child being brought up in Jamaica, I would regularly be asked, 'What do you want to be when you grow up?' By the time I was in Year 6 of primary school, I knew exactly what I wanted to be. I wanted to be a teacher. Could it have been that my teachers made such an impression on me, that I was being influenced in this direction? They did make a big impression on me, so this was a strong possibility. A few years ago, I was invited to speak at an event in New York. My Year 6 teacher (who unknown to me was also visiting in New York at the time), had been invited to the event. So, for the first time in more than 40 years, we were going to be seeing each other. It was such a beautiful surprise and we have remained in touch. She brought along, to show me, all the years of newspaper clippings that she had collected about me. It was a wonderful reunion. Today, as I look back, I recall that while being at high school, I did set up my own 'home school'. This meant that on my return home every afternoon, I looked after two small children whose family were next-door neighbours, along with two younger cousins. I taught them to read and introduced them to numbers and basic maths. A change of direction away from teaching came at approximately fourteen years of age, when I had an overwhelming sense of being called to ministry. Women, of course, were not allowed then in ordained leadership within the Church. I therefore had no role models, but there was something I felt I was being drawn to, deep inside.

As a young child, Alexander Hamilton would have watched the other children around him going to school, and may even had known the reason why he had to be home-schooled (his parents were not married and back then children of unmarried parents were treated differently – so he was not allowed to attend the church-run school). We learn that he was a prolific reader and writer. And although his home life was exceptionally challenging, he would have been aware of those who were being treated differently, too. He would have been aware of those being enslaved and who had no voice. He may also have been aware of what was happening in America, and it is possible that even then, he was thinking about how to make the world as he knew it a better place. One gets a sense of his awareness of injustices and of him itching to make a difference; nurturing thoughts of not only doing something about the things he was seeing and experiencing, but changing the world to become a more just one for all.

SHARE AND DISCUSS

Discuss the following questions as a group.
(This is an invitation to share, within the group, lifelong ambitions; what inspired people? Did they follow through on their dreams?)

1. Can you remember as a child thinking or saying what you wanted to be when you grew up?
2. How easy or difficult was it to fulfil that ambition?
3. Who or what were some of those early obstacles?

Sometimes we read stories in the press or hear matters discussed on the news where an individual is referred to as being ambitious. I have even heard it said of the clergy, 'Oh, Revd "X" is very ambitious.' Here they are not referring to the person aspiring to achieve something noble; someone determined to bring something to fruition or make a difference. Instead, it is spoken of in a negative way. What they are really saying is that 'this person just wants to get to the top'. In other words, it is not the work that is motivating the individual – it is their ego! The question is, why do you want to get to the top, and what does 'get to the top' actually mean? How many people will you pass on your way to the top and what difference will it make, not only to you but to the wider community to which you belong? If it is just about getting to the top, then, what next? Is it possible that you arrive at the top, only to find it does not fill that gaping hole you feel inside? If there is no sense of satisfaction or no sense of being really fulfilled or making a difference, then where does this leave you with regards to having a sense of being driven by purpose?

BIBLE

Let us hear from Mark's and Luke's gospel about the disciples jostling for position.

Choose two different people to each read these two passages, with a short pause between each reading.

MARK 10:35–40
James and John, the sons of Zebedee, came forward to him and said to him, 'Teacher, we want you to do for us whatever we ask of you.' And he said to them, 'What is it you want

me to do for you?' And they said to him, 'Grant us to sit, one at your right hand and one at your left, in your glory.' But Jesus said to them, 'You do not know what you are asking. Are you able to drink the cup that I drink, or be baptized with the baptism that I am baptized with?' They replied, 'We are able.' Then Jesus said to them, 'The cup that I drink you will drink; and with the baptism with which I am baptized, you will be baptized; but to sit at my right hand or at my left is not mine to grant, but it is for those for whom it has been prepared.'

LUKE 9:46–48

An argument arose among them as to which one of them was the greatest. But Jesus, aware of their inner thoughts, took a little child and put it by his side, and said to them, 'Whoever welcomes this child in my name welcomes me, and whoever welcomes me welcomes the one who sent me; for the least among all of you is the greatest.'

Now that you have heard both passages twice, consider what words and phrases stood out for you and why.

THINK AND DISCUSS

Take around 15 minutes to discuss the following questions. If you are in a large group, it might be better to split into pairs or groups of three.

1. Did the disciples forget what they were about?
2. Was sitting to the right or left about positioning themselves?
3. What difference would it make as to who was the greatest?
4. What is the significance of using a child as an example to them?

Spend a moment to think about what it has felt like when you thought you deserved a promotion (or a position of importance, or that you really wanted) that was then given to someone else. Did it leave you feeling demoralised, with a bitter taste in the mouth, and if so, how did this express itself?

I have often asked myself, what possessed the disciples to be arguing about which of them would be the greatest? It is as if they had forgotten what being with Jesus was all about – a life of serving others! I wonder if it is possible that the disciples had lost their way and their sense of purpose and therefore no longer remembered why they were following Jesus. In the Gospel of Matthew, it is the mother of the two disciples, James and John, who is ambitious for her boys and made the request to Jesus on their behalf (Matt. 20:20–21). Today we refer to people who are overly ambitious for their children as 'helicopter parents'. This mother does not secretly make her request behind locked doors. She boldly drags her boys before Jesus and openly makes the request. I cannot help but wonder if her sons were embarrassed by this whole experience.

Alexander Hamilton arrived in New York from the Caribbean with a deep hunger to achieve as much as he could. This was not purely about bragging that he too could attain academic greatness within a short space of time (as did Aaron Burr). We get a sense that he genuinely wanted to make a difference; he not only wanted to see change happen, be on the fringe or be an observer recording the change (as much as he loved writing), he wanted to be part of the change; he wanted to be at the heart of the change that he hoped to see.

WATCH

In our first clip for this session, you will hear Hamilton referring to himself as a 'diamond in the rough' trying to reach his goal, and he agreed that like his new adopted country, he was 'young, scrappy and hungry'. He linked up with like-minded friends for a cause – The Revolution – rebelling against the demands of King George. But there was another cause – freedom for those enslaved. In the words of his friend, Lauren: '… we'll never be truly free until those in bondage have the same rights as you and me…' Hamilton had a social conscience. He would have remembered the discomfort he felt as a child, seeing humans being trafficked and enslaved. Now he was older, he was in a hurry, he did not want to waste time. Now he could finally make a difference.

Show video clip of the song 'My Shot'.

The young revolutionaries' ambition was not about self-gratification; they were young, dashing and impressionable, but were not about to waste their time lying around. How much easier it would have been to go backpacking, see the world, just simply having fun with no responsibilities, exploring this new land, with no adults to boss him around. This would have been familiar territory for Alexander Hamilton because it would appear that during much of his childhood, he entertained himself. One of the things he did was to develop his habit of reading which, along with writing, stood him in good stead. Although only a new arrival in the USA, he was up to speed with the political narratives being played out, chief of which was England's overtaxing of the new colony. Perhaps he saw this as another form of injustice being played out, triggering all the feelings that he had as a child. Back then he was powerless and had things done to him, decisions made for him – where he should live and who he should live with. Now, he was no longer a child; he was going to try to do his bit to create the change he wanted to see. I would like to believe that in all of this, too, he had a sense that history was in the making. In his words, 'Don't be shocked when your history book mentions me, I will lay down my life if it sets us free ...'

There was no doubt that there were many around him who went with the status quo – happily paying whatever tax was being demanded and continuing to enslave other human beings. They may have been discontented but did not have the courage to 'rise up'. It is possible that they thought it would all go away in its own time. I believe that in every circumstance we face, the key is knowing what the best response is that we can give. I am reminded of the parable of the rich fool (Luke 12:16–21):

Then he told them a parable: 'The land of a rich man produced abundantly. And he thought to himself, "What should I do, for I have no place to store my crops?" Then he said, "I will do this: I will pull down my barns and build larger ones, and there I will store all my grain and my goods. And I will say to my soul, Soul, you have ample goods laid up for many years; relax, eat, drink, be merry." But God said to him, "You fool! This very night your life is being demanded of you. And the things you have prepared, whose will they be?" So it is with those who store up treasures for themselves but are not rich towards God.'

This individual was wealthy, but he had no sense of purpose. His business was doing well but he lacked vision and purpose. He lacked a sense of direction – he also lacked 'a cause'. He thought that accumulating more and more would perhaps make people look up to him. His ambition was simply to build bigger barns to store the larger harvest. Having an ambition to create great wealth cannot be an end in itself. 'Greed' is the word that comes to mind, and if we are not careful our life becomes inextricably linked with the abundance of 'stuff' that we accumulate just for the sake of having more. Everything around us, advertisements in shops and elsewhere, entices us and seems to reinforce this message: 'Buy more, double what you have and you will be just great.' How should we be responding to the ongoing pressures to keep accumulating more and more? It does not make us happier or more secure. I wonder how many people were left hungry while this wealthy man hoarded what he had, without any sense of responding to the needs of those around him. If our identity is merely linked with our possessions and the status it brings, then this could have serious implications for our wellbeing and that of others.

The season of Lent is a good time for us to give some serious thought to our desire to constantly acquire more. It is a good time to interrogate ourselves, to ask, 'What are we overcompensating for?' – to ask questions about purpose and meaning for our lives. The writer of Ecclesiastes 3:12 says, 'I know that there is nothing better for them than to be happy and enjoy themselves as long as they live'. Accumulating stuff: designer bags, trainers, sportswear, all these things do not bring real happiness. A life lived in service and doing good deeds, challenging injustices and showing compassion, is what will bring a true sense of purpose to one's life. This Lenten period could be the time to rediscover our passion and redirect our ambitions and desires, thus enabling our real ambitions to become lifegiving to ourselves and all around us.

Temptation, which we also address during this second week of Lent, is most appropriate as it can also be entwined with doing just about anything to attain our ambition. It is possible that our first formal introduction to the word 'temptation' began when we were first taught the words of the Lord's Prayer as children: 'lead us not into temptation'. We are praying, asking that God – perhaps through the help of other people – may lead us away from those unwise decisions that, left to our own devices, we seem to be constantly drawn to. Some of us may be relieved that we did not 'go all the way' when we were tempted sexually. But Jesus had something to say about that: 'You have heard that it was said, "You shall not commit adultery." But I say to you that everyone who looks at a woman with lust has already committed adultery with her in his heart' (Matt. 5:27–28). Temptation is not really about what we do, it is about our state of mind, the thought process. Lent is a good time to address that, and to reflect on the things that occupy our minds, our thinking.

BIBLE

To help us address the theme of temptation, we will be reading a passage of Scripture from the second book of Samuel in the Old Testament.

Choose two different people to read this passage, with a short pause between the two readings.

2 SAMUEL 11:1–15

In the spring of the year, the time when kings go out to battle, David sent Joab with his officers and all Israel with him; they ravaged the Ammonites, and besieged Rabbah. But David remained at Jerusalem.

It happened, late one afternoon, when David rose from his couch and was walking about on the roof of the king's house, that he saw from the roof a woman bathing; the woman was very beautiful. David sent someone to inquire about the woman. It was reported, 'This is Bathsheba daughter of Eliam, the wife of Uriah the Hittite.' So David sent messengers to fetch her, and she came to him, and he lay with her. (Now she was purifying herself after her period.) Then she returned to her house. The woman conceived; and she sent and told David, 'I am pregnant.'

So David sent word to Joab, 'Send me Uriah the Hittite.' And Joab sent Uriah to David. When Uriah came to him, David asked how Joab and the people fared, and how the war was going. Then David said to Uriah, 'Go down to your house, and wash your feet.' Uriah went out of the king's house, and there followed him a present from the king. But Uriah slept at the entrance of the king's house with all the servants of his lord, and did not go down to his house. When they told David, 'Uriah did not go down to his house,' David said to Uriah, 'You have just come from a journey. Why did you not go down to your house?' Uriah said to David, 'The ark and Israel and Judah remain in booths; and my lord Joab and the servants of my lord are camping in the open field; shall I then go to my house, to eat and to drink, and to lie with my wife? As you live, and as your soul lives, I will not do such a thing.' Then David said to Uriah, 'Remain here today also, and tomorrow I will send you back.' So Uriah remained in Jerusalem that day. On the next day, David invited him to eat and drink in his presence and made him drunk; and in the evening he went out to lie on his couch with the servants of his lord, but he did not go down to his house.

In the morning David wrote a letter to Joab, and sent it by the hand of Uriah. In the letter he wrote, 'Set Uriah in the forefront of the hardest fighting, and then draw back from him, so that he may be struck down and die.'

Now that you have heard the passage twice, consider what words and phrases stood out for you and why.

THINK AND DISCUSS

Discuss the following questions as a group.

1. **What were the signs of David's sense of entitlement that led him to make the kind of choices he did?**
2. **What role was played by others' collusion in this tragedy?**
3. **Someone at the top being engaged in major deception – how does this impact on the wider community?**

David's soldiers were at war with the Ammonites and normally the king would have been with his soldiers. On this occasion, however, David had stayed home. He appears rather restless. We learn that he caught a glimpse of Bathsheba, the wife of one of his foot soldiers, and that he desired her! David seizes the opportunity and brings Bathsheba into his bed. The woman becomes pregnant. To cover up what he has done, David tries to manipulate the solider, but when that doesn't work, orchestrates the situation for Uriah to be on the frontline – and unsurprisingly he is killed in battle (v. 17). Instead of planning for the war, King David's energy becomes focused on himself and his lustful desires. It would be true to say that he had a choice but that he chose incorrectly and with detrimental consequences to himself and those around him.

I recently attended the 50th wedding anniversary celebrations of a well-known couple within the Jamaican diaspora. They are a couple who work very hard in the community, catering for many functions large and small. It was a beautiful service of thanksgiving followed by a reception with the menu covering many of the Jamaican recipes of old. There was much joy shared on that day. And yet, sadly we know that thousands of marriages are dissolved, with adultery cited as the reason for the break-up. I was surprised to read in a recent survey that Christians involved in extra-marital affairs still believed that what they were doing was wrong. Where unfaithfulness contributes to the breakdown of a marriage, we have to ask, as we would in this Old Testament story, 'Did the person not recognise that the path they were going down was a disastrous one, not only personally, but for their family and the wider community of which they were a part?'

Things done in secret have a way of getting into the open. In the musical, Alexander Hamilton is away from his family and is under enormous pressure at work, and one may excuse his initial liaison as an error of judgement, due to the pressures he was facing. It does appear, though, that this affair turned into an ongoing relationship, revealing to us a person with deep inner struggles. I am reminded of the passage from Paul's letter to the church in Rome. Here, Paul says, 'I do not understand my own actions. For I do not do what I want, but I do the very thing I hate. ... I can will what is right, but I cannot do it. For I do not do the good I want, but the evil I do not want is what I do' (Romans 7:15, 18b–19). Hamilton clearly had a similar sense of an inner struggle too. In this description from the musical, his inner struggle is laid bare as he tries to resist the woman's advances.

WATCH

Here is a clip from the musical. In this clip, Hamilton is clearly wrestling with the temptation in front of him.

Show video clip of the song 'Say No to This'.

I cannot help but wonder if things would have turned out differently had Hamilton joined his family on their trip away. Or better still, if he had acted responsibly and not been so naïve in spending time alone with Maria Reynolds. I have often pondered on the merits of the saying, 'It is not a sin to look at the cake in the sweet shop window, it only becomes a problem if you eat it.' I have struggled with this, and Jesus actually did challenge this kind of thinking in his now famous Sermon on the Mount, as we read in Matthew 5, above. Jesus is not just signalling here. He is making it clear that the sin we commit does not begin and end in the wrong actions we indulge in. It begins in the passing thought, which we do not name and discard; instead, we nurture these thoughts until we get to the point when the opportunity arises, and we act on them. So, we keep walking past the cake shop even though we recognise this to be a temptation, admiring the cakes, pretending we are strong, strong enough to withstand the temptation – until something takes us into the shop. We are overwhelmed by our senses of smell, sight (now that we are at an even closer proximity) and taste, and before long, we find ourselves eating the cake!

When we ignore or leave unchecked the variety of sinful thoughts that surface from time to time, we are giving room for that sin to grow within. It will only be a matter of time before it morphs into something that could be deeply damaging.

Not only did this liaison damage Hamilton's marriage, but it led to attempted blackmail by people who were once his close friends. Aaron Burr, James Madison and Thomas Jefferson, former friends, were also tempted to use their knowledge of his liaison to blackmail him into making decisions that agreed with the kind of direction they wanted him to take. I struggle personally about Burr being involved in this plot when he himself had been in a long-term relationship with an 'English Officer's wife' – and had even had a child with her! And yet here he is, with others, using this same scenario to punish his one-time friend.

Not wanting to be in debt to them, Hamilton made the decision to go public about the affair, sharing the details of the relationship without understanding the consequences of his actions. His almost single-minded ambition to succeed and create well-needed change drove him to a place where he failed to recognise the temptation from within which was knocking him off course.

Lent is a good time for us to explore what it is that is driving our ambitions, ensuring that we do not yield to temptations that will destroy us and that which we are seeking to build.

REFLECTION

As this second session draws to a close, let's pause and call to mind our own journeys of ambition. Some of us may breathe a sigh of relief and say, 'Thank God I am not ambitious!' Benjamin E. Mays said that 'The tragedy of life doesn't lie in not reaching your goal. The tragedy lies in having no goal to reach.' So, what have those goals been that we have been trying to attain? Have we been tempted to go off the beaten track to get there quickly? I once asked a young boy in Hackney what he wanted from life. He began to tell me what his mother wanted him to be. 'Stop,' I said. 'I want to know what you want to be and do.' He paused briefly and said, 'Anything that makes lots of money.' I looked at him, sadly. I said, 'Young man, you're going to sell drugs.' I was even sadder when he did not contradict me. Hamilton achieved so much but was always on the edge.

PRAYER

The Lord is my Pace-setter, I shall not rush;
He makes me stop and rest for quiet intervals.
He provides me with images of stillness,
which restore my serenity.
He leads me in the ways of efficiency
through calmness of mind,
and His guidance is peace.

Even though I have a great many things
to accomplish each day,
I will not fret, for His presence is here;
His timelessness, His all importance,
will keep me in balance.
He prepares refreshment and renewal
in the midst of my activity
by anointing my mind
with his oils of tranquility.
My cup of joyous energy overflows.
Surely harmony and effectiveness
shall be the fruits of my hours;
for I shall walk, in the pace of my Lord
and dwell in His house forever.

Toki Miyashina (based on Psalm 23)

Together, each in our own language, let us say the prayer Jesus taught us:

Our Father, who art in heaven, hallowed be thy name; thy kingdom come; thy will be done on earth as it is in heaven. Give us this day our daily bread; and forgive us our trespasses as we forgive those who trespass against us; and lead us not into temptation but deliver us from evil. For thine is the kingdom, the power, and the glory. For ever and ever. **Amen**.

ACTION

In the light of what you have learnt this week, what will you do differently, or take forward?

PRAYER

Lord teach me to **strive to be in the room** where I can dream to make a difference, and handle the temptations that come along.

WEEK THREE

'*The unimaginable*':
Forgiveness and
Redemption

If you cannot forgive another, you burn the bridge
over which you yourself must pass.
GEORGE HERBERT

PRAYER

Dear Lord, we your children daily stand at this crossroad before the cross. May we be reminded that this is not a symbol of artistry, or a simple piece of jewellery gifted to us to be admired. Help us to move from being onlookers at the cross, to becoming active participants living out the meaning of the outstretched arms – forgiveness and redemption, borne out of love. **Amen**.

INTRODUCTION

I grew up at a time when I would regularly hear the adults around me saying, (for us to hear, of course), 'Children must be seen and not heard', and they meant it! So, as they casually gathered under the large almond tree – with its branches giving enough protection from the sun while its large leaves swayed just enough to provide the well-needed breeze – we would anchor ourselves just within reach of hearing the adults' exchanges of life stories. It was on one such occasion that I remember hearing stories of hurt, and the women, each unconsciously trying to outdo the other regarding the level of pain experienced, using the emphatic phrase, 'I will never forgive *him*.' Occasionally, it was, 'I will never forgive *her*.' As a small child, listening in to adult conversations, it would have been totally unacceptable for me to join in, even if what I had to say was worthy to be heard. I do recall at the age of eight, thinking about the words of the Lord Prayer, 'Forgive us our trespasses, as we forgive those who trespass against us.' Sitting amongst the others were churchgoing women. I waited to hear their admonishment about the need to forgive, but this was not forthcoming.

The story of *Hamilton* presents us with a self-assured young man who is convicted about the rightness of the path he is on. 'Swords no doubt would have clashed' and insults would have been exchanged, not unlike the febrile Brexit atmosphere here in the United Kingdom. Working as the chaplain in our Westminster Parliament, I was consciously aware of the bonds of friendships being stretched to breaking point. Parliamentarians and members of the public were seen to be digging their heels in to their respective corners. Encouraging them to find a middle ground where they could meet was almost impossible. In this kind of atmosphere, words and actions are exchanged that leaves a sense of hurt and anguish. In the musical production, Hamilton has one of many such exchanges with Samuel Seabury who was keenly in favour of the king's rule; Hamilton tells him: 'My dog speaks more eloquently than thee.'

The old saying, 'sticks and stones can break my bones, but words can never harm me' is not entirely true. Hidden scars from hurtful words often take longer to heal, especially as we tend to hold on to or nurse the wound after it has been delivered. Using another analogy, we 'stoke the fire': we find friends who agree with our point of view, thus giving us the ammunition to continue hating or being angry and enraged.

In our liturgical confessions, we confess the sins we have committed in 'thoughts, words and deeds' whether through a moment of 'negligence, weakness or a deliberate act'. My husband loves to eat toast and rarely cleans up the crumbs. The crumbs, over the years, have been a source of deep irritation to me. Each time I challenge him, however, he says, 'I did not leave them there on purpose, Rose.' This somehow adds to my irritation. His sin of negligence continues to be a recurring theme in our 37 years of marriage! I am learning to daily practise the art of forgiveness, thus enabling us to enjoy our life together. Reading this, you might think there is nothing to be forgiven here. But, in our relationships, it is the recurring little things that if not addressed become the 'straw that breaks the camel's back'. Perhaps if we practise the art of forgiveness in the small things, it might just be easier to receive God's grace for the 'big' things that impact us.

SHARE AND DISCUSS

Discuss the following questions as a group.
(This is an invitation to share, within the group, experiences of when people have forgiven someone, or have themselves been forgiven.)

1. **Can you remember a time when you were hurt by something that was said or done to you?**
2. **Or have you done or said something that caused another to feel hurt?**
3. **Did you find it easy to forgive them, or did they forgive you? How did that leave you feeling?**

In my previous role as a parish priest preparing families for baptism, I was keen to regularly share with them that the baby being brought forward for baptism would learn the important tenets of the Christian faith by seeing it at work in the lives of their parents, grandparents and godparents. So, as they grew, they would learn for example about forgiveness when they saw those closest to them saying sorry, being forgiven, and relationships restored; they would learn about compassion when they heard those closest to them react and respond to refugees, the homeless and the most vulnerable in society. There is a great burden of responsibility that weighs on the shoulders of all who profess to be Christians to practise the faith and thereby live in a Christlike manner. Perhaps this is what Jesus was referring to in Matthew 18:6: 'But whoever causes one of these little ones who believe in Me to sin, it would be better for him if a millstone were hung around his neck, and he were drowned in the depth of the sea' (NKJV). Very strong words, one may say, but it does highlight the responsibility that comes with naming ourselves as Christians.

I can still recall at the age of fifteen being told by an adult family member that I should not have shared information about getting a holiday job with my friend, as it meant they too would have access to extra income. Looking back, I can see that this was just selfishness by the adult, but at the time it left me confused because I had thought I was doing something kind. I concluded that as a Christian, I had done the right thing. I did not dare tell them this, though; they were the adult, and I was the 'child'. Culturally it would have been inappropriate for me to correct them. I could only hope that they would come to recognise that what they said to me was wrong. Adult Christians run the risk of confusing younger or fledgling Christians if we do not live out the tenets of the faith we profess. At the heart of the Christian faith is the cross of Jesus Christ, and this is all about forgiveness. Our faith only becomes real when it is lived, and practising forgiveness is an expression of that. The apostle Paul in 2 Corinthians 5:7 reminds us that 'we walk by faith, not by sight'. By sight, we see all the wrong things and avow to avenge, not to forgive – on the other hand, by faith we recognise as Christians our connection to the cross and we allow ourselves to be caught up in the Spirit's call to 'Let the same mind be in you that was in Christ Jesus' (Phil. 2:5). In other words, our attitude should be like that of Christ, having 'the same mind, having the same love, being in full accord and of one mind' (Phil. 2:2). Even on the cross Jesus was still forgiving: 'Father, forgive them;

for they do not know what they are doing' (Luke 23:34).

This brings into question the thinking that we can only forgive where there is genuine apology. I do remember saying to my children when they were at primary school, 'That sorry does not sound as if you mean it! Say it again, and this time I want you to say it as if you really are sorry.' This may work with small children, but we cannot force someone to apologise or to say sorry. The reality is that our forgiveness is not about the other person. God did not wait for us to say sorry before forgiving us. This is what Paul had to say in Romans 5:8: 'But God proves his love for us in that while we still were sinners Christ died for us.' God took the initiative. Consider the energy consumed in having to remember on a regular basis that someone has done us wrong. The reality is that this can easily consume us, harming us in the process; leaving us embittered, changing our personality. Imagine the possible sense of freedom if we did not have to wait for them to come to us and say sorry. I am reminded of the words of Jesus in his Sermon on the Mount: 'So when you are offering your gift at the altar, if you remember that your brother or sister has something against you, leave your gift there before the altar and go; first be reconciled to your brother or sister, and then come and offer your gift' (Matt. 5:23–24). The longer we take to attend to our broken relationships, the more it eats us up inside and therefore interferes with our relationship with God.

BIBLE

Let us now hear from Matthew's gospel what Jesus had to say on forgiveness, when Peter, his disciple, asked how many times we should be forgiving others.

Choose two different people to read this passage, with a short pause between the two readings.

MATTHEW 18:21–35

Then Peter came and said to him, 'Lord, if another member of the church sins against me, how often should I forgive? As many as seven times?' Jesus said to him, 'Not seven times, but, I tell you, seventy-seven times. For this reason the kingdom of heaven may be compared to a king who wished to settle accounts with his slaves. When he began the reckoning, one who owed him ten thousand talents was brought to him; and, as he could not pay, his lord ordered him to be sold, together with his wife and children and all his possessions, and payment to be made. So the slave fell on his knees before him, saying, "Have patience with me, and I will pay you everything." And out of pity for him, the lord of that slave released him and forgave him the debt. But that same slave, as he went out, came upon one of his fellow-slaves who owed him a hundred denarii; and seizing him by the throat, he said, "Pay what you owe." Then his fellow-slave fell down and pleaded with him, "Have patience with me, and I will pay you." But he refused; then he went and threw him into prison until he should pay the debt. When his fellow-slaves saw what had happened, they were greatly distressed, and they went and reported to their lord all that had taken place. Then his lord summoned him and said to him, "You wicked slave! I forgave you all that debt because you pleaded with me. Should you not have had mercy on your fellow-slave, as I had mercy on you?" And in anger his lord handed him over to be tortured until he would pay his entire debt. So my heavenly Father will also do to every one of you, if you do not forgive your brother or sister from your heart.'

Now that you have heard the passage twice, consider what words and phrases stood out for you and why.

THINK AND DISCUSS

Take around 15 minutes to discuss the following questions. If you are in a large group, it might be better to split into pairs or groups of three.

1. **How might forgiving someone release us from the pain of carrying the hurt?**
2. **Should we only forgive when there is a 'genuine apology', and who decides if it is genuine?**

The rabbis suggested forgiving one another at least three times. Peter, however, talking with Jesus suggested seven times (the number 7 carries a particular significance in the Jewish religion: God resting on the seventh day after the work of creation (Gen. 2:2); Noah brings seven pairs of clean animals into the ark (Gen. 7:2); in the interpretation of Pharoah's dream there is seven years of plenty and seven years of famine (Gen. 41); there are seven days to the feast of the Passover (Exod. 13.3-10); around the years of Jubilee there is a seven-year cycle (Lev. 25); seven demons were driven out of Mary Magdalene (Luke 8:2); in the feeding of the 4,000, it is seven loaves that are multiplied and seven baskets that the leftover food is collected into (Matt. 15:32–37) so maybe Peter was showing off when he used the number 7, increasing what the teachers of the law suggested. Jesus' response, however, 'Not seven times, but … seventy-seven times' is pointing us in the direction of 'the unimaginable'. God's forgiveness knows no boundaries or conditions. It is this kind of forgiveness that we are being called to practise.

WATCH

This week's first video clip from the musical focuses on Eliza's pain as she wrestles not only with Hamilton's infidelity but the way in which he brings shame to her and the family as he, in trying to prove that he did not fraudulently use public funds, tells the whole world the details of his extra-marital affair.

Show video clip of the song 'Burn'.

There is nothing sugar-coated about engaging with the reality of forgiving someone who has wronged us or done us harm. Whilst serving in Hackney as a parish priest I was moved by the words of a mother whose 16-year-old son had been murdered by another boy who was just 14 years old. During the trial, she remarked on the sadness she felt on top of the pain she was already feeling at the loss of her son, that this 14-year-old had no family present with him in court. I was blown away by this comment. What generosity! But we need to own the fact that sometimes forgiveness does not come easily. I recall a practising Christian leader withdrawing from ministry with the words, 'I cannot forgive those who murdered my child.'

In this video clip we have just viewed, Hamilton's wife, Eliza, expresses her distress: 'You told the whole world how you brought this girl into our bed. In clearing your name you have ruined our lives … You forfeit all rights to my heart … I hope that you burn.' These are strong words. When we feel that someone has broken our trust or that indeed, our trust has been taken for granted, that we have been betrayed – the anger and rage cannot be underestimated. The question is, how can we own these feelings of rage and yet with the help of the Holy Spirit, be guided to the place of forgiveness? The reality is that the more space we give to this rage, the longer we hold on to it, the less space there will be for forgiveness to enter and find a place to dwell.

BIBLE

Let's look at another passage of Scripture, this time from the Old Testament. It is the well-known story of Joseph, whose jealous brothers sold him into slavery. Time passes, and he is reunited with his brothers and his father. His father, Jacob, eventually dies and we meet the story where the brothers are afraid that Joseph may still be holding a grudge.

Choose two different people to read this passage, with a short pause between the two readings.

GENESIS 50:15–21
Realizing that their father was dead, Joseph's brothers said, 'What if Joseph still bears a grudge against us and pays us back in full for all the wrong that we did to him?' So they approached Joseph, saying, 'Your father gave this instruction before he died, "Say to Joseph: I beg you, forgive the

crime of your brothers and the wrong they did in harming you." Now therefore please forgive the crime of the servants of the God of your father.' Joseph wept when they spoke to him. Then his brothers also wept, fell down before him, and said, 'We are here as your slaves.' But Joseph said to them, 'Do not be afraid! Am I in the place of God? Even though you intended to do harm to me, God intended it for good, in order to preserve a numerous people, as he is doing today. So have no fear; I myself will provide for you and your little ones.' In this way he reassured them, speaking kindly to them.

Now that you have heard the passage twice, consider what words and phrases stood out for you and why.

THINK AND DISCUSS

Discuss the following questions as a group.

1. **Was there real regret by Joseph's brothers, or were they only concerned about themselves and how they would survive now that their father had died?**
2. **How might forgiveness in action become the glue that keeps families together?**

The story of Joseph and his siblings is more than just about jealous brothers behaving in an unbrotherly fashion. They meant harm to come to their brother, and they did not care about the grief of their father at the loss of a much-loved youngest son. Their selfishness took priority over the bonds of brotherhood and the reality that they were part of one family. In Joseph's response to them after the death of their father, he made it clear: 'I know you intended to harm me, but God has used it for good.' How is it that brothers who thought they had the upper hand found themselves living in a manner that was full of fear?

They had been afraid that their father would find out about how they disposed of their youngest brother, pretending he had been attacked by 'a wild animal' (Gen. 37:20, 31–33). This would mean having to ensure that it was a closely guarded secret.

When Joseph first recognises his siblings, he does not reveal himself to them. Instead, he orchestrates the moment when he will do this. In chapter 45 of Genesis we read:

> Then Joseph could no longer control himself before all those who stood by him, and he cried out, 'Send everyone away from me.' So no one stayed with him when Joseph made himself known to his brothers. And he wept so loudly that the Egyptians heard it, and the household of Pharaoh heard it.

There were tears from the brothers' side too. We are told that they were 'dismayed' (v. 3), but throughout they are reassured by Joseph. 'Do not be angry with yourselves,' Joseph tells them. 'You may have done what you did to cause me harm by selling me, but I want you to know that God was the one who was sending me ahead of you in preparation for this famine.' So in verse 7 we read: 'God sent me before you to preserve for you a remnant on earth, and to keep alive for you many survivors.' Joseph seems to go the extra mile in reassuring his brothers. So the brothers who meant him harm are not only forgiven but find themselves redeemed – restored to an even better place where 'brotherly love' is warmly expressed.

WATCH

The second video clip also speaks to us of Hamilton's redemption that brings him back to the fold.

Show video clip of the song 'It's Quiet Uptown'.

Not only has Alexander Hamilton's sinful behaviour broken the bonds of the relationship with his wife, but politically he is also a broken man and when you think it could not get any worse, their son Philip dies in a duel! From all this anger, rage, deep pain and heartache, comes redemption. Hamilton and Eliza's relationship is restored. In the words of the song, 'They are trying to do the unimaginable.' Words from the lines sung by Angelica, Eliza's sister, are most poignant: 'There is a grace too powerful to name, we push away what we can never understand, we push away the unimaginable.'

I would like to suggest that the 'grace' being referred to is that made possible through the death of Jesus Christ on the cross, making what in our eyes appears unimaginable, possible. Left to our own devices we would feed and nurse the wounds of hurt, anger and rage at the circumstances around us, and especially those directly impacting on us. Many people find their energy wrapped up in unforgiveness.

However, God's grace freely given keeps knocking at the door of our hearts. So many of us refuse to open our hearts and take a great big leap, receiving God's grace and moving into that space of redemption.

A pawn shop is a familiar sight on most high streets, and most of us understand what it means to 'redeem' an item, thus having it returned to its rightful place. The word 'redemption' comes from the same root. It means that we purchase something; but we do more than just purchase it – it is removed completely from that place. Jesus' death on the cross was the price paid for our sins. 'For God so loved the world that he gave his only begotten son, that whoever believes in him should not perish but have everlasting life' (John 3:16). Jesus' death on the cross has made it possible for us to be removed from the place of turmoil, from hardness of heart and the spirit of unforgiveness. Jesus' death on the cross is the ransom paid, that we might be free from all that captures us and seeks to hold us bound. In the movies, when a ransom is paid then the person being held gets to go free. So, in 1 Peter 1:18–19 we read:

> You were not redeemed with corruptible things, like silver or gold … but with the precious blood of Christ, as of a lamb without blemish and without spot. (NKJV)

We connect to this grace and experience this redemption through the forgiveness made possible by God's forgiveness of us through the cross. We are confronted by this grace with a need for us to consciously respond with thankfulness and our own need, having 'freely received, to freely give' (see Matt. 10:8). Hamilton's relationship is restored, and he can now be seen with Eliza, 'side by side'; there is some solace in this restored relationship and the environment in which they are now in. In the light of God's grace freely bestowed on us, we no longer need the hustle and bustle of the noisy places around us. Instead, there is something to be said of listening for the 'still small voice' (1 Kings 19:12 NKJV) – the kind of stillness that allows us space for reflection and informs us for the future.

REFLECTION

As we draw this session to a close, in silence let us individually think about or call to mind those who over the years have wronged us, and those we may indeed have wronged. Perhaps we can own to ourselves the people we are holding in our hearts, struggling to forgive. Might we be ready to let them go – to forgive them? Might we be ready this Lent to go in peace to someone (a family member, a work colleague, or an acquaintance) who behaves in an antagonistic manner towards us? If we are not able to meet face to face, might we be prepared to find a way symbolically to acknowledge God's grace in our lives, the source of forgiveness and redemption?

PRAYER

Lord Jesus, please walk with me along the journey of life; through trials and tribulations, walk with me. When I am tempted not to forgive, remind me of your grace and your willingness to forgive me. Help me to pray with meaning, the words you taught us: 'Forgive us our trespasses, as we forgive those who trespass against us.' Help me to remember, Lord, the need for me to practise forgiveness day by day. **Amen**.

Together, each in our own language, let us say the prayer Jesus taught us:

Our Father, who art in heaven, hallowed be thy name; thy kingdom come; thy will be done on earth as it is in heaven. Give us this day our daily bread; and forgive us our trespasses as we forgive those who trespass against us; and lead us not into temptation but deliver us from evil. For thine is the kingdom, the power, and the glory. For ever and ever. **Amen**.

ACTION

In the light of what you have learnt this week, what will you do differently, or take forward?

PRAYER

Lord, teach me to **strive to be in the room** where forgiveness and redemption is daily sought after.

WEEK FOUR

'We'll bleed and fight
for you':
Love and Sacrifice

JOHN 15:13

Greater love has no one than this: to lay down one's life for one's friends. (NKJV)

PRAYER

Lord of life and love, open our eyes that we may see the generosity of your love bestowed on us. Enlarge our hearts to show compassionate love to our fellow humans across the globe, and enable us to lovingly care for your creation. Teach us to pattern your unconditional and sacrificial love so that together we may transform your world. **Amen**.

INTRODUCTION

The Oxford dictionary defines love to be 'an intense feeling of deep affection'. However, in almost all the weddings that I have officiated at (possibly approaching 100 since I began in ministry), I have deliberately drawn to the attention of the couples the fact that nowhere in the ceremony do we speak of love as a feeling! This is in stark contrast to popular culture. Love songs in the pop world often refer to love as a feeling or speak of 'falling' in love. So, for example we have 'it feels like, it feels like I'm in love'; or there is 'When I fall in love, it will be for ever...' Love has also been defined as 'a strong and lasting affection between spouses and lovers who are in a happy, passionate and fulfilling relationship'. I want to suggest, however, that love is much more than a feeling that is shared intimately between two lovers. There is the love between parents and their children; love between siblings; love between friends or work colleagues. The reality is that love is a vital part of human existence, and this is long before we begin to attach it to feelings of intimacy.

There is something also to be said about love being a necessary part of life to be a truly thriving community or to be fulfilled as an individual within that community. If we think back to 1989, there were images coming out of Romania, showing a country on its knees, with its Communist leader, Nicolae Ceauşescu, apparently casting aside those who were most vulnerable in that society. Investigative news teams had managed to get into the country and their cameras were showing us images of 'unwanted' children supposedly being cared for in institutions where they were fed, albeit basically, but had very little love or expressions of emotional and psychological warmth shown to them. They were simply left rocking in their cots or their beds and sometimes chained to the physical structures around them. Not being able to receive love through the medium of emotional care and physical touch, in other words, not receiving any real expression of love, clearly impacted deeply on their psychological, emotional and physical wellbeing.

We have heard from songwriters who have put music to the words 'love makes the world go round'. And it does, because it acts as the necessary glue or thread that holds a community together. Within the Torah (the first five books of the Old Testament – the Jewish Scriptures), it was the purpose of the Ten Commandments to hold the community together. It is therefore most interesting that when the Pharisees, who were the religious leaders of the day, asked Jesus which was the greatest of the commandments, to see how he would respond, he drew together the commandments focusing on love. Here is the question put to Jesus in Matthew 22:36–40:

> 'Teacher, which is the greatest commandment in the Law?' Jesus replied: '"Love the Lord your God with all your heart and with all your soul and with all your mind." This is the first and greatest commandment. And the second is like it: "Love your neighbour as yourself." All the Law and the Prophets hang on these two commandments.'

Jesus not only summarises the Ten Commandments, but he further underlines that which he believes to be the greatest, adding a second one which he describes as not dissimilar to the first, instructing us that everything hangs on both these. We are therefore to love God with our whole being and we are to love our neighbours as we love ourselves (love God, love ourselves and love others). I note that in Deuteronomy, we are to love God with all our strength too (Deut. 6:5), in other words, with everything. There is no real argument as to God's sacrificial love for us – the cross of Christ is there to prove it. Those memorable words of John 3:16 comes to mind: 'For God so loved the world that he gave his only Son...' God's love simply cannot be called into question, but our love for God is certainly more questionable. I know that I regularly fall short of this. Embarking on any Lenten journey, including this one, is about finding a pathway to enable us to deepen our love for God. And for that love, in turn, to flow out to those who we daily interact with. I am reminded of what is written in 1 John 4:20; how can we say we love God whom we have not seen and do not love our brothers whom we can see?

SHARE AND DISCUSS

Take around 15 minutes to discuss the following questions. If you are in a large group, it might be better to split into pairs or groups of three.

1. Can we truly love others if we do not love ourselves?
2. Is it selfish to love ourselves, or is loving ourselves crucial to our understanding of Christ's love in us?
3. What are the signs that real love is in place, and should feelings play a large part in this?

BIBLE

We will now read from John's gospel about an interaction Jesus had with his disciple Simon Peter.

Choose two different people to read this passage, with a short pause between the two readings.

JOHN 21:15–19

When they had finished breakfast, Jesus said to Simon Peter, 'Simon son of John, do you love me more than these?' He said to him, 'Yes, Lord; you know that I love you.' Jesus said to him, 'Feed my lambs.' A second time he said to him, 'Simon son of John, do you love me?' He said to him, 'Yes, Lord; you know that I love you.' Jesus said to him, 'Tend my sheep.' He said to him the third time, 'Simon son of John, do you love me?' Peter felt hurt because he said to him the third time, 'Do you love me?' And he said to him, 'Lord, you know everything; you know that I love you.' Jesus said to him, 'Feed my sheep. Very truly, I tell you, when you were younger, you used to fasten your own belt and to go wherever you wished. But when you grow old, you will stretch out your hands, and someone else will fasten a belt around you and take you where you do not wish to go.' (He said this to indicate the kind of death by which he would glorify God.) After this he said to him, 'Follow me.'

Now that you have heard the passage twice, consider what words and phrases stood out for you and why.

THINK AND DISCUSS

Take around 15 minutes to discuss the following questions. If you are in a large group, it might be better to split into pairs or groups of three.

1. **In his questioning, do we get a sense that Jesus may have doubted Simon Peter's love?**
2. **Do we have doubts about declared love by significant others in our lives?**
3. **Do we share any empathy for Simon Peter's frustration?**

I have often wondered what Jesus meant when he said, 'Do you love me more than these?' They were at the seaside, and this was Peter's old 'stomping ground'. Could he have been referring to the fishing trade? With all the equipment visible by the beach, could he be wondering if Peter would give up the preaching ministry and return to fishing? After all, this was an area he knew well enough. It could be that Peter is being asked if he is prepared to say goodbye to the fishing industry. Jesus may also have been referring to the other disciples: 'Peter, do you love me more than your fellow disciples?' Being back with the disciples in this intimate setting, sharing a meal, the memory of Peter's denial may have resurfaced. If his courage failed back then, what would keep him strong now? He is asked about his love a third time, and it could be that being asked three times mirrors the three times Peter denied Jesus. Now, though, instead of denial, he can have a lasting memory of declaring his love for Jesus.

For Peter and for us, simply saying 'I love you' is not enough. Peter is given some work to do: 'Feed my sheep.' There is a responsibility that comes with loving – there is work to be done and there is a sacrifice to be made. As Christians seeking to follow Christ, we will need to understand what it is that we are being asked to do in response to the question, 'Do you love me more than these?' We will need to work out what we leave behind as well as what we take on.

In the musical we find in Alexander Hamilton a young man with a great survival instinct. His unorthodox beginnings still left him with a sense of himself as a person with the capacity to be loved and to love, although there is a confession to Angelica, his sister-in-law, that he is always seeking more and is never satisfied. We do not get a sense that he ever masters the deep longing that he has inside or that he knew for sure what he was lacking. We are presented, however, with someone who is a work in progress. This he probably knew. His love for those around him appears to be conflicted, so although he swears undying love for Eliza, there is some emotional connection between him and Angelica which, though acknowledged, we are never sure is acted on by either of them. His interaction with his wife, Eliza, is tender but occasionally firm in sticking to the agenda of that which he is seeking to accomplish.

I feel personally drawn to this historical figure and am convinced that the reason for this is because he 'wears his heart on his sleeve'. He is vulnerable but not afraid to be in the mix. He is, in Jamaican parlance, 'bombastic' – edgy, boastful – but in a kind of innocent way. He is simply telling the story of who he is; he is keen to get the message out: 'This is who I am, and this is where I am coming from and this is what I have achieved, and can go on to continue achieving, with the right level of support around me; I will grab hold of every opportunity that comes my way.'

In any kind of relationship, I guess important questions are: Do we allow ourselves to 'fall' too easily 'in love', get carried away, and just depend merely on what we are feeling at a particular time and place? Should we be taking stock, weighing up the cost of that love and the sacrifice it is likely to require for that relationship to be a thriving and fulfilling one? King George III failed to understand the sacrificial nature of love and somehow thought that he could threaten and bully the arrivals to the new world to fall in line with his request.

WATCH

In the first video clip for this session, we catch a glimpse of King George's unacceptable behaviour wrapped up in the guise of 'love'. Contrast this with the second clip in this section where Hamilton and Eliza have a moment of connection and open their hearts to each other, displaying real vulnerability.

Show video clips of two songs: 'You'll Be Back' and 'Helpless'.

It is true to say that Hamilton, in this second clip, clearly lays on the table who he is – he's not wealthy (not even a dollar to his name); he's been living without a family since he was a child. In this song we capture something of the vulnerability of Alexander Hamilton. I am surprised by his level of self-awareness when it comes to matters of the heart. I feel really connected both with the song and with the Hamiltons' predicament. As a child growing up, my father was 'around' physically but was emotionally detached. This may have been due to his own childhood fleeing from Fidel Castro's Cuba with his mother and siblings; his mother later becoming mentally unstable and the children being left to grow themselves up – to survive.

Hamilton describes quite an unsettled childhood that resonates with my own. My mother left for the UK when I was approximately two years old. I do remember growing up having a deep longing and an aching within me for something that I knew was missing. I did not actually remember my mother so I could not really say that I was missing her, and on the other hand, I could not, at such a young age, articulate what that longing was for. However, I was deeply involved with the local church where I worshipped weekly, and it was here that I felt the love of an 'adopted' mum and dad – two individuals unconnected to each other (this was not a legal adoption), but two people who loved me as good parents would love their own child. In their expression of love, I interpreted it as God's love being expressed through them. Unknown to them, they became the medium of a very deep love which fulfilled that aching within me. It did not take me long to recognise this as a gift to me and to respond positively in return.

In this second video clip, we get a sense that Hamilton recognises that this love between him and Eliza is something special. His childhood was so very different, though. It was the opposite of the kind of settled family upbringing that Eliza had experienced with her sisters, who we see she is still close to. Hamilton wanted this relationship with his wife, and he wanted more than ever to do what he could to make it work. The memory of what happened to his mother was still strong. He speaks of not forgetting his mother's face as he promises not to leave Eliza feeling helpless.

In the process of leading marriage preparation sessions, or during relationship counselling, I would ask couples from time to time to think about whether the love they thought they had for each other meant that they needed to be together or sacrificially refrain from coming together. Of Hamilton and Eliza, one could ask if they had given enough time in reflection on whether they were right for each other. What would they both need to give up, to sacrifice, so that they could create a lasting happy home environment?

Often in the Old Testament story of sacrificial offering, the people are asked to give animals that are 'without defect' (for example, Num. 19:2). In other words, our love offering is about giving of our best; giving to God what is right and not from what can be regarded as our leftovers – giving to each other not things we don't want, things we deem to be useless or no longer good enough for our own purpose, but things that still carry meaning for us. I believe we will know when we give to God and each other from a place of genuine love, because we will see that we are contributing towards a flourishing and sustainable relationship.

BIBLE

Let us now look at a well-known passage of Scripture from Paul's letter to the church in Corinth.

Choose two different people to read this passage, with a short pause between the two readings.

1 CORINTHIANS 13
If I speak in the tongues of mortals and of angels, but do not have love, I am a noisy gong or a clanging cymbal. And if I have prophetic powers,

and understand all mysteries and all knowledge, and if I have all faith, so as to remove mountains, but do not have love, I am nothing. If I give away all my possessions, and if I hand over my body so that I may boast, but do not have love, I gain nothing.

Love is patient; love is kind; love is not envious or boastful or arrogant or rude. It does not insist on its own way; it is not irritable or resentful; it does not rejoice in wrongdoing, but rejoices in the truth. It bears all things, believes all things, hopes all things, endures all things.

Love never ends. But as for prophecies, they will come to an end; as for tongues, they will cease; as for knowledge, it will come to an end. For we know only in part, and we prophesy only in part; but when the complete comes, the partial will come to an end. When I was a child, I spoke like a child, I thought like a child, I reasoned like a child; when I became an adult, I put an end to childish ways. For now we see in a mirror, dimly, but then we will see face to face. Now I know only in part; then I will know fully, even as I have been fully known. And now faith, hope, and love abide, these three; and the greatest of these is love.

Now that you have heard the passage twice, consider what words and phrases stood out for you and why.

THINK AND DISCUSS

Discuss the following questions as a group.

1. Does this passage set too high a bar for us to achieve?
2. 'Love never fails' (v. 8, NKJV) – how real is this statement in the light of the many breakdowns of relationships that we see?
3. How does it feel to know that we are being called to act from a higher place?

This is a passage which reminds us that however important we think our roles, all that we do is useless unless it comes from a place of real love. It is not enough for us to simply talk about injustices that we see around us or to respond in a superficial way (forming a committee that simply does more talking). Action is needed, and the right kind of action, too, that is going to make a difference. The New Testament Church spent a significant amount of time arguing as to whether the Gentiles who committed to following Christ should be circumcised. If only they could remind themselves of the words of the prophets encouraging them to change the emphasis and focus instead on circumcising their hearts (Jer. 4:4). The apostle Paul is also at pains to point out to the church in Rome that their fussing about circumcision is about showing outward signs only. What is more important is the cutting away from our hearts the things that prevent us from truly loving God and each other (Rom. 2:29).

So much harm has been done in the past when

thousands took on missionary endeavours to bring Christ to the so called 'heathen' world. And still today, in the name of 'preaching the gospel' we continue to do so in a vacuum where we show no signs of love to those we are apparently trying to win for the kingdom of God. I am aware of many Christians who mistakenly say they know the will of God on certain topics and then proceed to behave in an unChristlike manner, such as walking out of church, refusing to speak to or to have a meal with their fellow sister or brother in Christ, simply ostracising those who happen to hold a different view to the one they hold. This behaviour is certainly not from a place of love, and neither is it patterning God's generosity. To pattern God's generous love is to do the opposite to what the world says. We are to turn the other cheek, we are to respond in love, we are to forgive continuously. It is perhaps in doing so that we will get to that place where we will see with our own eyes that truly 'love never fails'.

WATCH

In the next clip, Burr and Hamilton are addressing their firstborn children, Theodosia and Philip. These two very different men discover that they do share something in common – it is a sacrificial love for their offspring.

Show video clip of the song 'Dear Theodosia'.

In this clip, the word from both men speaks of a love so deep that they talk of sacrifice – 'we'll bleed and fight for you' is one of the promises they make. They share their commitment 'to lay a strong foundation' and of doing whatever it takes to ensure they have a better world than the one they inherited. I understand what it is that drives these two men. I am conscious of the fact that I overextend myself, and why? I too want my children and my grandchildren to be part of a new and much better world, where they will be allowed to flourish as part of the one human race and not be pre-judged in a negative way due to their ethnic background or the colour of their skin. I want my grandchildren to live in a world where they can see images of themselves in all walks of life. I want my granddaughters to be safe in both the daytime and in the evening. I want my grandsons to walk through any community and not be stabbed on the one hand or suddenly become a suspect on the other. I want them to be able to apply to any educational institution or for any job they aspire to, and know that they will be equally assessed.

I wonder which bit of the song you were moved by. Culturally we live in a world that pretends that men are either not in touch with their emotions or are incapable of showing emotion. I would like to suggest that where this is a reality, it is because we have socialised our men and boys to turn off their emotions. I have been lucky in my 39 years of ministry to connect with men, young and old, who, without being coerced, were ready to express what was being felt within them.

When I was in the parish where I first served as an ordained minister, I took a call from the local funeral director. They explained that someone who was not from the parish wanted me to officiate at his wife's funeral. I had officiated at his mother's funeral six months previously (she lived in the parish). His wife, forty years old, had died suddenly of a heart attack while they were entertaining friends at a barbecue at home. He was insisting that it had to be me who officiate. I recognised the name and agreed to see him. About 30 minutes later he turned up at the church office. He was a big guy, over 6 ft tall. I opened the door to him, and he stepped in. He stood, filling the frame of the office door, and simply wept. I held him and hugged him till the tears subsided, assured him I would do the service, but agreed that I would get the relevant information from him at another time when the emotions would be less raw. When I next met with him, now more composed, he spoke vividly of the love they shared and how shattered he was at losing her. I remember being touched by his openness, an unusual trait in a male. He was talking to me about the depth of the love that they shared and how he wished he could have taken her place. Such love! It was clear that this love was inexplicably deeper than mere feelings.

The word used when talking about God's love is *agape* and it means not only God's love for us but the way we, in turn, respond to God and to each other in the light of God's love – this is, in effect, 'unconditional love'. It was this unconditional love that sent Jesus to the cross, 'while we still were sinners' (Rom. 5:8). It is this kind of unconditional love that we are being constantly called to pattern.

Paul's first letter to the Corinthian church tells us that 'Love is patient, love is kind ... it keeps no record of wrongs' (1 Cor. 13:4–5). I mentioned in an earlier chapter about the crumbs my husband leaves after eating toast. Whenever he pleads innocence, a part of me so wants to get a little notebook out to show him how many times he has left the surface full of crumbs! But then this Corinthian passage comes to mind – love 'keeps no record of wrongs'. He is saved by the bell, or should I say by the apostle Paul? I can genuinely say this is a work in progress as I do mention it less often at times (more noticeably when having a low moment), but I dare not keep a written record!

If our suffering is necessary to help someone, then might we in the name of God's love, consider it? I am reminded of those in Germany who hid Jews from the Nazis, or those who helped the Jewish children to escape from what would have been certain death. I think also of an elderly man who prior to the

COVID-19 pandemic, and when he was well, would go to hospital during visiting hours – those elderly people who he noticed had no visitors, he would approach and speak with them, sacrificially giving his time to others. I was inspired by his love for others and all the time, seeking nothing in return.

REFLECTION

What have been the times in our lives when we have loved another or felt loved, unconditionally?

PRAYER

I have always found the words of the prayer below moving:

> Thanks be to thee, O Lord Christ, for all the benefits which thou hast given us; for all the pains and insults which thou hast borne for us.
>
> O most merciful redeemer, friend and brother, may we know thee more clearly, love thee more dearly, and follow thee more nearly; for thine own sake.
>
> **Richard of Chichester, 1197–1253**

Together, each in our own language, let us say the prayer Jesus taught us:

> Our Father, who art in heaven, hallowed be thy name; thy kingdom come; thy will be done on earth as it is in heaven. Give us this day our daily bread; and forgive us our trespasses as we forgive those who trespass against us; and lead us not into temptation but deliver us from evil. For thine is the kingdom, the power, and the glory. For ever and ever. **Amen**.

ACTION

In the light of what you have learnt this week, what will you do differently, or take forward?

PRAYER

Lord, teach me to **strive to be in the room** where I can learn and see what love is.

WEEK FIVE

'The story of tonight':
Hope and Courage
through Adversity

*Teach us to look, in all our ends, on thee for judge,
and not our friends; that we with thee, may walk
uncowed by fear or favour of the crowd.*
RUDYARD KIPLING (1865–1936)

PRAYER

Dear Lord, may we be empowered to boldly participate in life instead of waiting unengaged in the challenges of daily living; give us grace that we may find joy, friendship and fellowship in the people and places which others have long abandoned; and give us courage that we may go unfrightened across the waters where you bid us come. **Amen**.

INTRODUCTION

Living through a pandemic, most of us would confess that there have been times of deep concern (or worry) as to where this may all end, not just for us and our families individually, but as a society and as a wider world. For many of us, there was a stop to our normal routine and the many things and people we took for granted. There was rarely a sound of the all too familiar echo, 'This is the way we have always done it!' as we reluctantly realised that our once-treasured rulebook was being prised from our grasp and being thrown out. So, how are we to navigate this 'new world' that we find ourselves a part of? Are we to spend countless hours locked away in fear, due to the circumstances we find ourselves in, or might we just step out and courageously navigate each obstacle we face in our daily journey? I am reminded of the words attributed to Dorothy Bernard, 'Courage is fear that has said its prayers.' This clearly means that for those of us with faith, we go forward not in a foolhardy or non-committal way, but with the kind of prayerful consciousness that enables us to be hopeful about the journey that lies ahead and each step we take on that journey.

SHARE AND DISCUSS

We are now in the fifth week of Lent, the week before Holy Week and Easter. How might we explore hope and courage through adversity as we make our journey towards the so called 'crunch moments' to get to Easter?

Share briefly (two or three minutes per person) some of the really difficult moments that you have had to face during the period of the COVID-19 pandemic. It is possible that such an experience may have enabled you to recall childhood memories of hard times.

As you share your stories, seek to identify moments of hope and some of the courageous steps taken along the way.

When my second daughter was in Year 6 of primary school, we were sitting on the sofa watching a news programme discussing famine in Ethiopia, when she suddenly said to me, 'Mummy, the children at school are laughing at me and calling me poor.' I asked her, 'Darling, why are they calling you poor?' She replied, 'Because I am not wearing Nike trainers. And Mummy, they bring the shoebox to show the price of their trainers: £70!' I looked at her for a moment and surprised myself by responding calmly. I said, 'Darling, you will have to find a way of coping with what they are saying because Mummy will never spend such a large amount of money buying footwear that you will outgrow in a short space of time.' I continued, 'Did you see the people who were starving just now on the television? They have nothing to eat. Apart from their families, they have nothing. Those people are poor. You are not poor. So you will just have to cope with their silliness. Maybe you can tell them about what you have just seen for yourself.' I then hugged her and reassured her of my love – but it was a love that would not be buying her expensive footwear!

Here in the Western world, we can all think of situations where when we talk about experiencing poverty, we are really referring to *relative* poverty. So, measurement of poverty may include the lack of computers (and please be assured that I am not denying or wanting to talk down the fact that poverty does exists here in the West; also, for example, children being hungry in the school holidays when school lunches are unavailable – hence the Marcus Rashford campaign, etc.). We have often heard it said, 'How can we, the fifth richest country in the world, accept the level of poverty that we are seeing at present on our streets and in some of our cities?' Sadly, being a child of the Caribbean, I wish that I could say with confidence where on the rich-list we are as Caribbean countries, but I suspect that it is a long way off.

The island of Nevis is the alleged birthplace of the young Hamilton in the eighteenth century. It is a place where many are trying to make a living; a place where there are no filters – so a child born out of wedlock is ostracised and even the Church colludes with this behaviour, excluding that child from joining the church school, as if they had done something wrong themselves. This causes the young Hamilton to be educated privately, and even at this early age, we catch a glimpse of someone who is driven. Although he suffers the loss of a mother, and a stepfather who takes his mother's wealth because the law entitles him to do so – leaving the young boy penniless – he dares to live in hope and to dream of a future. And not just any future, but a future where he may contribute and make a difference.

BIBLE

We will now read from Mark's gospel a story depicting hope and courage through adversity.

Choose two different people to read this passage, with a short pause between the two readings.

MARK 9:14–29

When they came to the disciples, they saw a great crowd around them, and some scribes arguing with them. When the whole crowd saw him, they were immediately overcome with awe, and they ran forward to greet him. He asked them, 'What are you arguing about with them?' Someone from the crowd answered him, 'Teacher, I brought you my son; he has a spirit that makes him unable to speak; and whenever it seizes him, it dashes him down; and he foams and grinds his teeth and becomes rigid; and I asked your disciples to cast it out, but they could not do so.' He answered them, 'You faithless generation, how much longer must I be among you? How much longer must I put up with you? Bring him to me.' And they brought the boy to him. When the spirit saw him, immediately it threw the boy into convulsions, and he fell on the ground and rolled about, foaming at the mouth. Jesus asked the father, 'How long has this been happening to him?' And he said, 'From childhood. It has often cast him into the fire and into the water, to destroy him; but if you are able to do anything, have pity on us and help us.' Jesus said to him, 'If you are able! – All things can be done for the one who believes.' Immediately the father of the child cried out, 'I believe; help my unbelief!' When Jesus saw that a crowd came running together, he rebuked the unclean spirit, saying to it, 'You spirit that keeps this boy from speaking and hearing, I command you, come out of him, and never enter him again!' After crying out and convulsing him terribly, it came out, and the boy was like a corpse, so that most of them said, 'He is dead.' But Jesus took him by the hand and lifted him up, and he was able to stand. When he had entered the house, his disciples asked him privately, 'Why could we not cast it out?' He said to them, 'This kind can come out only through prayer.'

Now that you have heard the passage twice, consider what words and phrases stood out for you and why.

THINK AND DISCUSS

Take around 15 minutes to discuss the following questions. If you are in a large group, it might be better to split into pairs or groups of three.

1. In what way was the father of the boy expressing hope?
2. How would you describe the real adversity being experienced?
3. Mark's gospel says this was accomplished only

by prayer, and Matthew's gospel speaks about faith (Matt. 17:20). What does this mean?

Imagine being the parent of such a child with an illness that leaves not just the child but the whole family ostracised. In recent years, although much is being spoken of more openly about mental illness, we still hear of incidences where people are shunned or treated less well by the wider society, including the police, due to being mentally unwell. We have heard credible stories of how lockdown during the pandemic has increased people's lack of mental wellbeing, including stories of an increase in eating disorders. This has affected a wide range of age groups. Family crises may have impacted on some, pushing them over the edge too. I believe that one of the main lessons from this reading is a reminder that getting through some of the adversities that we face means that something extra is required. Prayer and faith! Could this be what others refer to as resilience?

Looking back at my own life growing up in the Caribbean, I recognise the many adversities that I faced and have come through. I can only say for sure that my life of prayer (and prayers by many others on my behalf) and faith played a huge part in me overcoming those adversities. My strong faith in a God who loves me enough to sacrifice his Son filled me with real courage and hope to keep going. Repeatedly in the *Hamilton* musical we hear the question asked, 'How does a bastard, orphan, son of a whore go on and on, grow into more of a phenomenon ... be seated at the right hand of the father [Washington]?' This is, of course, the same Alexander Hamilton (11 January 1755/57–12 July 1804) now referred to as being a statesman, lawyer, politician, banker, one of America's Founding Fathers. And from a poor and humble beginning.

WATCH

Let us listen to this first clip for this session where Aaron Burr, his long-time friend who later becomes his enemy, reflects on his friend's rise to infamy.

Show video clip of the song 'Non-Stop'.

There is something special about Hamilton that his friends and especially Aaron Burr just cannot put their finger on. His wife, too, reminds him of his humble beginnings: 'Look at where you are, look at where you started, the fact that you are alive is a miracle.' In other words: 'That you have come through the adversities you have and still not only be alive but thriving is nothing short of a miracle!' The refrain, 'How do you write like you're running out of time' reflects the fact that there is no stopping him – he is grabbing life with both hands. Perhaps it could be said that he, more than any other, was more than conscious of the thin line between life and death and therefore wanted to make sure he accomplished all that he could in his lifetime. And what a contrast this was to his friend Aaron Burr who, when challenged by Hamilton to take a stand, simply said he 'wanted to wait and see which way the wind will blow'.

How engaged are we with life, or daily living? Or can we be referred to as 'bystanders', watching life go by as we blame circumstances for the fact that we have not achieved our goals, or fulfilled our ambitions? At a very young age, I learnt to depend on something deeper than I could see with the naked eye. I had entrusted myself to God, and this God had seen me through some tough challenges. I therefore knew that if I was going to get through each day, month and year, I had to keep putting my trust and my faith in God. Prayer became my regularly used mantra – several times per day (the more formal prayers being longer) – communicating with my creator, liberator and friend. Here in my diocese of Canterbury, one of the four priorities that I have set for us to focus on is prayer. I believe that prayer keeps us in tune with our creator God and reminds us that we must look deeper than our physical selves – we reach into the soul and draw on something deeper that gives us purpose and abundant life.

In the passage of Scripture we read earlier, the disciples appeared not to be able to assist the boy and his father. 'Why couldn't we have done what you did?' they asked Jesus privately. Jesus tells them that faith and prayer is needed. This is not magic, or the disciples' say-so. There is something deeper at play. This is something that we are constantly growing into day by day as we stay close to Jesus, becoming confident and trusting disciples. We are reminded in Paul's letter to the church in Ephesus that faith is a 'gift of God' (Eph. 2:8-9). Prayer speaks volumes of our dependence on God; in prayer, we ask God to fill us with the gift of faith so that in believing we may see him at work in and through our lives and the lives of others, for whom we pray and whose lives we touch.

For our second Bible reading this week we go to the sometimes overfamiliar story of the cross echoed in even more familiar hymns and songs such as:

> On a hill far away stood an old rugged cross
> The emblem of suff'ring and shame;
> And I love that old cross where the Dearest and
> Best
> For a world of lost sinners was slain.
> **George Bennard (1873–1958)**

> There is a green hill far away
> without a city wall,
> where the dear Lord was crucified,
> who died to save us all.
> **Cecil Frances Alexander (1818–95)**

> Were you there when they crucified my Lord?
> Were you there when they crucified my Lord?
> O sometimes it causes me to tremble! tremble!
> tremble!
> Were you there when they crucified my Lord?
> **Charles Winfred Douglas (1867–1944)**

BIBLE

Let me try to capture the story of the Passion narrative before it gets to this week's selected passage. We find Jesus having a meal with his disciples – the Last Supper, during which holy communion is instituted; he prayerfully agonises in the garden of Gethsemane in anticipation of what is about to happen; he is betrayed and arrested, after which, he is tried and is sentenced to death. In this passage, we meet Jesus on the cross:

Choose two different people to read this passage, with a short pause between the two readings.

LUKE 23:32–43

Two others also, who were criminals, were led away to be put to death with him. When they came to the place that is called The Skull, they crucified Jesus there with the criminals, one on his right and one on his left. Then Jesus said, 'Father, forgive them; for they do not know what they are doing.' And they cast lots to divide his clothing. And the people stood by, watching; but the leaders scoffed at him, saying, 'He saved others; let him save himself if he is the Messiah of God, his chosen one!' The soldiers also mocked him, coming up and offering him sour wine, and saying, 'If you are the King of the Jews, save yourself!' There was also an inscription over him, 'This is the King of the Jews.'

One of the criminals who were hanged there kept deriding him and saying, 'Are you not the Messiah? Save yourself and us!' But the other rebuked him, saying, 'Do you not fear God, since you are under the same sentence of condemnation? And we indeed have been condemned justly, for we are getting what we deserve for our deeds, but this man has done nothing wrong.' Then he said, 'Jesus, remember me when you come into your kingdom.' He replied, 'Truly I tell you, today you will be with me in Paradise.'

Now that you have heard the passage twice, consider what words and phrases stood out for you and why.

The same crowds who thronged him on Palm Sunday, shouting 'Hosanna' (Matt. 21:9) made up the crowds who also shouted, 'Crucify him!' (Mark 15:13–14) and created false accusations about him (Matt. 26:59–60a). Jesus, however, showed much courage through adversity. It was as though he knew he was in his Father's hands, and even in this situation of being jeered at and cursed, we are presented with a Jesus who was calm and at peace. In the words of the songwriter, 'They crucified my Lord, and he never said a mumbalin word' (Traditional Negro spiritual).

THINK AND DISCUSS

Discuss the following questions as a group.

1. If we were in Jesus' position, would we have remained quiet?
2. What have we learnt from the passage?
3. What does the manner of Jesus' death tell us about our need to be risk-averse?

Jesus was clearly being made an example of publicly

by the manner of his death – being dragged through the streets and hung outside the city walls for everyone to see. In the eyes of those who condemned him, he is stripped of his kingdom and yet, in a way that the world cannot fathom, he is embracing his new kingdom through his death. Here we find him inviting others into his kingdom – a kingdom that no one can remove from him, however hard they try. Here one on the cross next to him cries out, 'Jesus, remember me when you come into your kingdom.' Jesus replies to the thief, 'Today, you will be with me in Paradise.' The dying criminal showed courage and hope too: courage to own who he was and take responsibility for his actions, and the hope that he would be forgiven and drawn into the fold. Having dared to act, he found himself rewarded. I wonder what difference it may make to our lives if we believed in Jesus enough (even at the last minute) to pray in a similar way to the thief on the cross: 'Lord, remember me when you come into your kingdom.' What if we were to chant this meaningfully, as a prayer – 'Jesus, remember me; when you come into your kingdom' – day by day? The words of the hymn writers Nahum Tate (1652–1715) and Nicholas Brady (1659–1726) may speak much to us here:

> Through all the changing scenes of life,
> in trouble and in joy,
> the praises of my God shall still
> my heart and tongue employ.

I cannot help but wonder about the impact of this on our lives and the lives of thousands, as we face the various challenges of life.

WATCH

Our final video clip captures the essence of Alexander Hamilton, the man with a story worth telling.

Show video clip of the song 'Who Lives, Who Dies, Who Tells Your Story?'.

Alexander Hamilton, this complex young man who experienced and escaped real poverty, did not take for granted the opportunity he had to start all over again. He remembered that where he was coming from created a life charting where he wanted to go. He was not afraid to take risks and would sometimes run towards the 'eye of the storm' partly out of naivety and partly from a place of integrity, all the time expressing through his actions that 'if you don't know what you'll die for, how will you know what you'll live for'. Through his vulnerability he presses on single-mindedly and rises to the top of government, making a lasting impact at the treasury, one that continues to serve the American people today.

The reality is the story of Hamilton, like the gospel of the Good News of Jesus Christ, is a story worth telling. But who should tell the story? I would like to suggest that those telling the story ought to be those who have met with Hamilton or, indeed, with Jesus. Those who have engaged with the characters in the story themselves will become the best storytellers because they will tell it from a place of 'real experience'. The disciples, having met and spent time with Jesus, were best placed to tell others about him. And that is why it was so disappointing when they could not heal the young boy. The expectation is, if you are in company with Jesus, then the ideals and way of life that he lived must be evident in our lives too.

Growing up attending Sunday School, I learnt the following song:

> Tell me the stories of Jesus
> I love to hear;
> Things I would ask him to tell me
> If He were here:
> Scenes by the wayside,
> Tales of the sea,
> Stories of Jesus,
> Tell them to me.
>
> First let me hear how the children
> Stood round his knee,
> And I shall fancy his blessing
> Resting on me;
> Words full of kindness,
> Deeds full of grace,
> All in the love-light
> Of Jesus' face.

William H. Parker (1845–1929)

I was lucky to have Sunday school teachers who could tell the story in words and song, and also through lived experiences. It made a difference. As a person of Afro-Caribbean roots, I am all too aware of the fact that the older generation in the community were of an oral tradition; that the elders carried the story of the history of the village or the nation. This would have been and is a huge responsibility for them to carry. Our responsibility was to be allowed to spend time with them and to learn it, as it were, by osmosis! Someone once said, Christianity is not taught, it is caught. I just love this idea! But what a huge responsibility it puts on those who profess faith to live it in such a way that it can be caught!

Just imagine how wonderful it would be if our children and grandchildren's generation caught faith from us. Caught it, because they heard us telling the story and caught it, because they saw us living the story of the Good News of Jesus Christ. Right now, the Church is experiencing a vacuum because we do not have enough storytellers who are confident enough to talk the talk and walk the walk when it comes to the message of the Good News. We have thousands of people who have been baptised and confirmed; thousands of people who have some connection with the Church but are, sadly, ill-equipped to tell and live the story.

The story of Alexander Hamilton is an old story of a founding father of the United States. But it is a story that came to life because one person, inspired by that story, was bold enough to find a new medium to share it through. At the wedding of Cana, found in chapter 2 of John's gospel, the adult Jesus comes on the scene. The wine served last is transformed and was known to be the better of the two wines served. Jesus himself, in his ministry, speaks about old wineskins being inadequate to hold the new wine (Matt. 9:17). We, the people of God, referred to by the Episcopal Presiding Bishop, Michael Curry, as the 'Jesus People', will have to ask ourselves how inspired and ready we are to be the new wineskins, telling the story of Jesus afresh, in a way that connects with a new audience. Every baptised and confirmed candidate must become confident champions of the story, living it and sharing it so that our changed lives become a conduit for others' lives to be changed.

The telling of the story draws us to a place of deep reflection on where we are coming from and where we need to be going. The Lenten discipline of study during the five weeks leading into Holy Week is meant to call us to fish in the deeper waters of life; to be rid of 'stuff' we no longer need for the journey, to travel light so that we can be ready and always fit for purpose and growing the kind of wisdom that comes from a lived knowledge of the story. Will you live and tell the story?

REFLECTION

As this final session, our time of sharing together during Lent, draws to a close, let us spend a moment reflecting on the story of Alexander Hamilton, and the story of the cross that we have been drawn into. How comfortable are we in this room, being challenged to live the story, that we might be better enabled to share the story – intentionally, inspiring others along the way?

PRAYER

Grant, O Lord, that amidst all the discouragements, difficulties and dangers, distress and darkness of this life, we may learn to depend on your mercy. Teach us to build our hopes on the solid rock of Jesus Christ, so that having this sure foundation we may become all that you desire us to be as your children, loving, forgiving, and full of hope and courage. **Amen.**

Together, each in our own language, let us say the prayer Jesus taught us:

Our Father, who art in heaven, hallowed be thy name; thy kingdom come; thy will be done on earth as it is in heaven. Give us this day our daily bread; and forgive us our trespasses as we forgive those who trespass against us; and lead us not into temptation but deliver us from evil. For thine is the kingdom, the power, and the glory. For ever and ever. **Amen**.

ACTION

In the light of what you have learnt this week, what will you do differently, or take forward?

PRAYER

Lord, teach me to **strive to be in the room** where I can reach for hope and courage daily, through all the adversities that I may face.